A Pe... Rose

To: Beyonce
Arline June Pearce

My first book of poetry
by
Arline June Pearce

A Peach Colored Rose

Copyright © 2002 by Arline June Pearce

Library of Congress
Cataloging in Publication Data

ISBN 0-7951-0342-5

Manufactured in The United States of America by
Watermark Press
6 Gwynns Mill Court
Owings Mills, MD 21117
410-654-0400

Sketches drawn by Arline June Pearce

Note: The silhouette sketch facing poem "Over the Years" was sketched from an original painting by Leo S. Carty's entitled "Friendship Path".

Arline June Pearce
ID #P2856925-235-4

20th Wedding Anniversary

Dedication

A Peach Colored Rose, my first book of poetry, is dedicated to the
memory of my beloved husband

Walter Norman Pearce, Jr.

<u>With special love to my children</u>
Richard W. Pearce
"Rich, I couldn't do it without all your computer assistance."
Noreen L. Pearce

<u>To my loving grand-children</u>
Michelle N. Kolpak
Christopher Longo
Casey Longo
<u>and sweet great grand-daughter</u>
Livannah Longo

To my grand-daughter Michelle N. Kolpak: "Being the oldest, you
have a special room in my heart. As you drift into the stream of life
and the river breaks through all barriers and tributaries; remember that
the mountain stays and follows you with my love."

A personal thanks to Marianne Romanetz Nucci, who said I would move on
when I was ready. With loving thanks for years of friendship and guidance.

Arline June Pearce

Table of Contents

Introduction

A Peach Colored Rose is Arline June Pearce's first book of poetry. Her poetry is no stranger to her family and friends. Since her teenage years, she used poetry as a form of expression. "My Piano" and "Slipping Away" are two poems she wrote as a teenager.

As a registered nurse, many poems were written and given to her patients. Many others were written for her family and friends.

Only a very "few" are willing to share feelings. Of that "few", a minuscule amount are willing to put these feelings in writing.

After the death of her husband and her retirement, she had <u>non-stop courage</u>, through a friend. The courage to express her feelings in poetry.

Someone once said, <u>"A bell isn't a bell until you ring it!"</u>. Arline June Pearce is ringing her bell.

What is Poetry?

Poetry is the gathering of words,
Placing the words in rhythm;
Then taking them for a dance.

May your heart travel across the years while reading my poems.

May you weave a tapestry of wonderful dreams to last forever.

Enjoy the rose-petal pages

Enjoy Mother-Nature, and

Old Father-Time will take care of everything!

My Mother's Flower

My mother's flower so choice and so fair,
Her peach-colored rose will always be there.
Although she has gone and time seems so long,
Her peach-colored rose stays forever strong.

Like a voice from the rose of long ago,
Whispering to and fro, I hear her say;
"Remember, the world in honoring you,
Will honor, dear heart, your mother, too."

The picture she traced stays with me yet,
The peach-colored rose, I'll never forget.

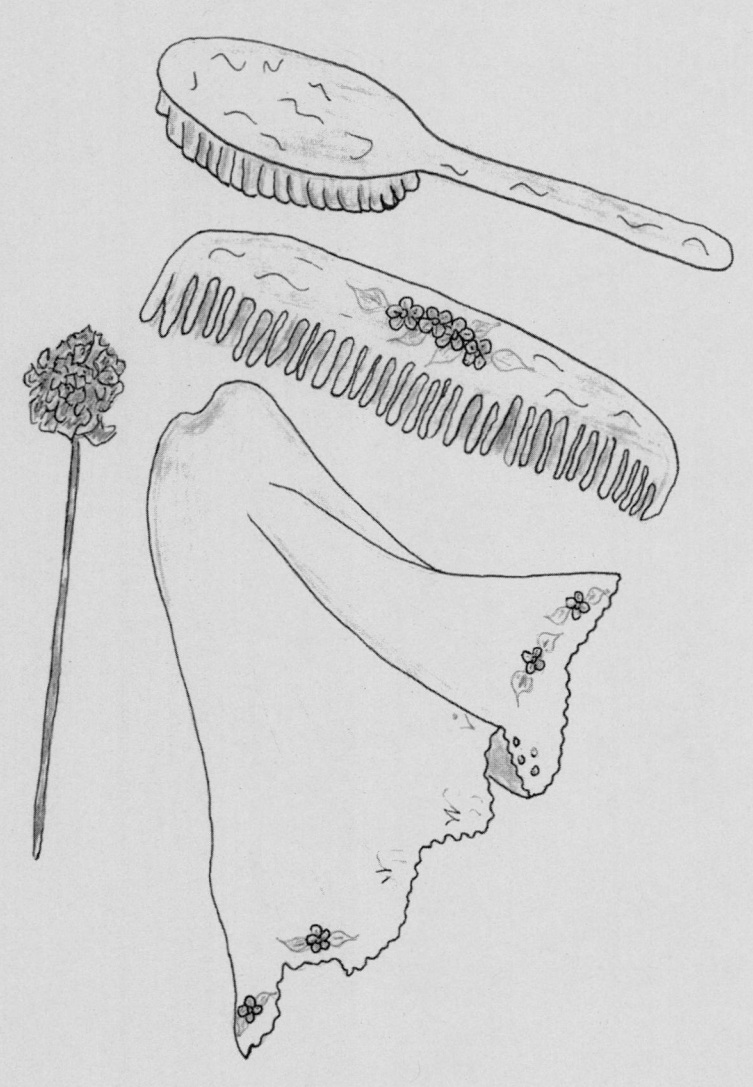

Traveling Back

It's nice to travel back now and then.
To feel the warmth my heart remembers when
A love enjoyed, akin to the verve of the sun,
And a feeling of always being so young.

On a December evening in 1952
I saw the love of my life, his eyes so blue,
We met in the 5 & 10 cent store,
Love at first sight, that's for sure.

His gazed blue eyes burned into mine
And laid silent claim so divine.
Not only on my body, but to the plains
And peaks and valleys of my spirit.

A great burst of heat rolled over me
Like a fireball of an unforeseen explosion,
Scorching my senses, he took my breath away
And stirred a powerful combustible ache
In the heart of my womb.

Like the birth of newly born flowers.
His gentle love showered those youthful hours
Whatever the years would bring
We always did, in our hearts, together sing.

Now my sorrow is so very deep
Like a cold, frigid, heavy rain
Soaking my clothes clean through
Covering my wilting body like a liquid skin.

On the 21st of February in the year two thousand
His last ardent breath exhaled with resound.
To leave me with a love which will never end.
He will forever and ever be my friend.

A Room Filled with Joy
Written for my new found friend, Susan.

It's only a short time since we met.
But friendship spans the void to let
You have a special place in my heart.
A room filled with joy never to part.

All the World is Mine

I have a dream, a fantasy -
To touch the enchanting art of time because this time,
this day, belongs to me.
Moment by moment, hour by hour, I gently float like a cloud.
And all the world is mine.
I can see what I loved. I can see what I left behind
In these stored treasures in my mind.
A creaking swing, footsteps on a stair, the phonograph
with records old and worn;
Jumbled scenes are shuffled all around as I touch
this enchanting art of time.
Mother smiling still like yesterday, her white-milk candy jar,
her doilies yellow and worn.
The sound of the noon-time dishes being cleaned away.
And all the world is mine.
Lace curtains, white as snow, washed with tender care.
I make them look their very best,
Allowing curtain-stretchers to do the rest.
The old train whistle echoes, then disappears as far
as the ear can hear.
The old iron rails with ties to hold them down are gone
as far as the eye can see.
Jumbled scenes are shuffled all around as I touch
this enchanting art of time.
I saw and loved and left behind these treasures in my mind.
This time, this day belongs to me. For all the world is mine.

Arline June Pearce

Class Reunion
Part 1 of 2

I sat beside my dresser drawer
Which held an invitation for
A class reunion. Class Fifty-one.
My goodness! I wanted to hide and run.

What might have been has changed to be
What truly is for me to see.
Wrinkles and weight I'd like to peel.
My dreams of perfection are much too real.

I sat and thought for just awhile,
I packed my head; maintained a smile
My mind filled with friendly places
Whose names recalled familiar faces.

I fell into an easy rhythm
Old songs and such filled my prism
Curiosity won my fear
For sure, I would attend this year.

I entered the room as if in space
Waiting for someone's warm embrace.
I stood and lingered just awhile.
To absorb each and every smile.

All over the room I could see
People indulged in memory.
Redefining what we had been
Comparing who we have become

Class Reunion
Part 2 of 2

Welcomed they did with open arms
Pictured name-pins lay out like charms
Was it a dove gliding through flight
That brought old dreams to me that night?

What fun it was to turn back pages.
Sharing past years through the ages.
We shared this time trying to win
And capture hearts so deep within.

Fidgety spouses fake a smile
Of teenage tales not their style.
Life has woven pieces of strand,
Into semblance of hearts so grand.

While driving home the moon was pale
I was a ship with my own sail.
The youthfulness that I once knew
Brought back old memories anew.

The scent that evening brought is mine
Sealed and bottled for all of time.
Whatever comes from that day's birth.
I'll treasure it, in all it's worth!

Arline June Pearce

Disruption of a Day-Dream

I want to save this very day.
I want to store it in a hide-away.
I'll find a hidden secret spot,
A place where even God forgot.

I'll write about a special time,
A special friend, a special find.
I'll write and savor every hour
Like a most delicate flower.

So years from now you'll look again
At how we walked and talked and then,
We listened to each others words.
We shared our hearts like chirping birds.

We journeyed in and out the streets
Until one brought us to our treats.
An antique shop with wooden floors
That welcomed us with opened doors.

It brought us back forgotten dreams.
The miracle of life it seems.
We browsed and strolled on creaky floors,
Beneath God's skies these antique stores

This day evoked a prophecy,
As we walked and shopped near the sea.
"But wait, what is that noise I hear?
The grandkids have arrived. Oh dear!"

Drop-by-Drop

It's hard to tell the moment when,
A friend becomes a friend and then
The friendship cup fills drop-by-drop
With tenderness that never stop.

Drops measure bits of keepsake dear.
That overflow to yesteryear.
Kind words of hope pour in this cup
To link each day without disrupt.

Drops like the grasp of one firm hand,
Or lips that say "I understand"
It's hard to tell the moment when,
A friend becomes a friend and then. . .

Dusk - The Saddest Time of Day

Dusk is like an illusion.
The sun
Is either above the horizon,
Or below the horizon.

Both day and night,
Are linked together.
They cannot do
Without each other.

Ironically,
They cannot exist
At the same time.
Dusk is the saddest time of day.

God's Paintbrush

It's as though
God dipped His paintbrush
into the sun;
Splashed you with sunshine,
And that sunshine
dispersed on me.

God's Pot-of-Gold

After the rain stopped
A beautiful rainbow-arch appeared
And trimmed the lace-like tree tops
With graceful wonder.

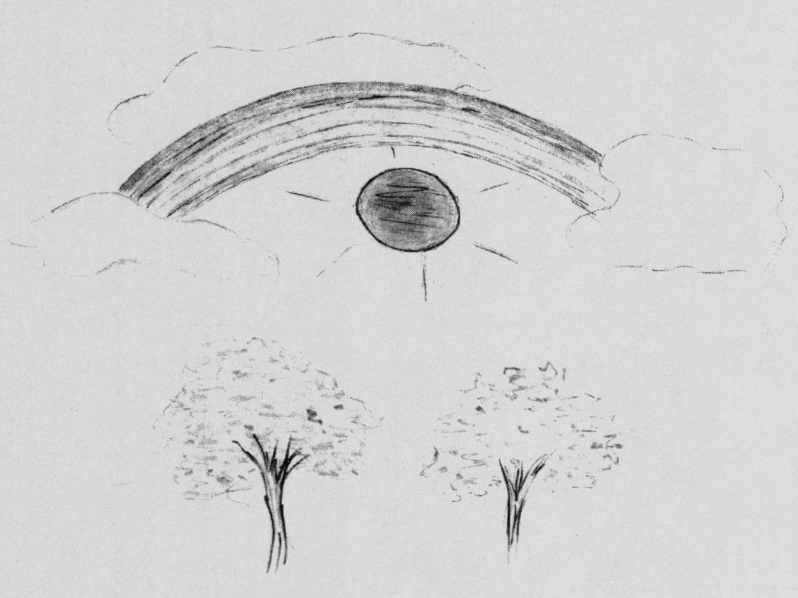

Arline June Pearce

Happiness is an Inside Job

Happiness is an inside job,
Where bright bouquets are mirrored in,
And deep compassion holds a sob.

To etch upon your soul and rob
A most engaging scene within.
Happiness is an inside job.

Rich, poor, young, old; you pound and throb.
You strive for higher goals to win
And deep compassion holds a sob.

Respect and admiration bob
To reach and touch that highest pin.
Happiness is an inside job.

Lives troubled pathways branch to swab
A myriad, days teeming as thin
And deep compassion holds a sob.

Beckoning like a swarming mob
Heaven bends low to catch again
Happiness is an inside job.
And deep compassion holds a sob.

I Caught the Shadows of Sunbeams

As the sun comes in and out
I watch the sunbeams
Dancing all about
Making shadows; giving dreams.

Like an offering in flight
The filtering rays
Alters my saddened plight
Into picture-post-card days.

I caught the lace-like shadows of sunbeams;
And turned them into beautiful dreams.

Life Has Been Brief

Life moves on, as you dream away.
Who knows upon what comes today?
The touch that lifts your soul divine
And teaches you His magic line.

No cunning rule, could ever reach,
Where soul's necessities find speech.
A sweet caress, or turning leaf.
You realize - Life has been brief!

Life's Journey

God gave me a journey in life.
He gave me the strength and the stamina
For the long and winding miles.
Above all,
God gave me the faith that makes me smile.

Mom's Treasures

Mom, it is your birthday today!
A special Mom, I'm proud to say.
Softer than waves across the sands,
Are the healing of mother's hands.

There's special moments in a day,
A breeze will blow a certain way.
A sound forgotten until then,
Drifts by to bring mem'ries again.

A screen door slamming far away,
The sound of dishes on a tray.
That's why I love the simple sights,
A rainbow after rain delights.

All take me to a younger time,
"All the world", as they say, "was mine".
The memories I left behind,
Forever treasures in my mind.

Mom, it is your birthday today.
A special Mom, I'm proud to say.
The greatest gift God ever planned.
Was you Mother, so dear; so grand.

My Cameo Pin

My cameo pin is bordered in gold.
A gem, they say, that gracefully grew old.
An engraved profile holds a warm smile,
As I bid her to stay for just awhile.

She is a treasure you cannot measure,
For all the years of her precious pleasure.
There are many things that do come and go,
But my cameo-love will only grow.

My Condo on the Beach
To my dear friend, Marianne, who has always been there for me

I love to reminisce in this place.
Such memories warm my soul and lighten my face.
Wherever else there may be,
My Condo is the solitude of me.
If I leave, I'll never part;
My steps may wander, but not my heart

My Gift of Love
A surprise gift from my dear friend, Marianne.

"A present?" I cried, "Especially for me?"
Quickly unwrapping so I could see
This gift the mailman brought today.
What could it be from so far away?

A necklace I saw, which hung like lace,
A tear-drop pendant for me to embrace
With a rose of love upon it's face.
What beauty - such art and loving grace!

Like a fragrance that lures me far away.
She gave me the smile of sunbeams in May.
I looked to God in Heaven above,
"Thank You for sending me this gift of love."

Arline June Pearce

My Magic Carpet

I shall proceed with gentle ease.
My Magic Carpet, if you please?

Her magic, my heart is knowing
Will have love, and new hope growing.
Her silent voice gives me delight,
Since my carpet, I did invite.

There will be miracles galore,
Such beauty, lying on my floor.
So warm, she beckons silently,
Inviting new found majesty.

Her bordered flowers open up,
Resembling sunshine in a cup.
Her flowers blossom endlessly,
And fill my heart with pageantry.

She whispers lowly and oh so chic.
Her flowers dance around and peek,
As if they're playing hide and seek.
She leaves a kiss upon my cheek.

And then invites me to her world.
Oh what a dream she has unfurled.
Her spell eases my restless heart
And girlish dreams will not depart.

I shall proceed with gentle ease.
My Magic Carpet, if you please?

My Piano

Piano chords, piano strings
Make you dance and make you sing.
The greatest gift ever planned
Is my piano, oh so grand.
No shooting stars, no lightning's source,
Piano playing is, of course,
To play the chords with fingers deep,
And waken Chopin from his sleep.
No matter what her tune does bring,
Piano gives me sounds of spring.

Old Secrets

Old secrets sprout tentacles,
That reach into every part of one's life
Catching the last elusive
Minutes of peace and strife.

Words once quivered in my heart,
Like the point of a poison arrow.
Piercing the shrill
Of a singing sparrow.

Now those same words dissolve,
And blow away in the breeze.
Whispering and fading
In the towering trees.

Old secrets sprout tentacles,
That reach into every part of one's life.
But my poems unburden my soul
My heart hemorrhages and rids the strife.

Arline June Pearce

On the Porch

My rocker swaying
In quiet rhythm
To the motion
Of a moonlit prism.

I swoon as the moon
In the night breeze
Climbs to the tops
Of the glistening trees.

Frisky crickets fidget
And fiddle a fine tune,
Free and easy
'Neath the summer moon.

The wind carries
A kiss of clover
Here on the porch,
When day is over.

A wish to each I tell!
Deep within
The core of life,
My heart remembers well.

Over the Years

Over the years I have had many friends.
Some stayed! Some have dwindled! Some disappeared!
You, my Marianne, stayed through thick and thin.
No distance; no time or even the space
Were ever an issue with you, my friend.

You'll never know how much you've done for me.
When hours seemed darkest . . . you lent an ear,
Yet leaving me free; and open as air.
Your loyalty and trust are tried and true.
It wasn't until I chanced one day and
Found a worthy and loyal friend like you.

No. We didn't grow up together.
Nor did I room with you in your college.
We did not meet until we were women.
You touched a chord in my heart from the start.
Thanks! Thanks to you - loyal and worthy friend.
Here's a toast to friendship: True to the end.

Retirement

Tomorrow the hustle and bustle will stop,
This is my day to rest and to pop
On that smile, and begin to play.
Everyone knows that this is my day.

My recipe as I wake each morn,
Will help me see the beauty adorn.
These things I promise and then,
I'll wake each day and start over again.

I'll take my love and sentiment,
Mix it with some cheer.
Then I'll add some kind thoughts,
For every day of each year.

I know the fun will come my way,
I'll see beauty with each and every day.
Days like lyrics of a song,
And tireless hours that tag along.

Tomorrow the hustle and bustle will stop.
This is my day to rest and to pop
On that smile, and begin to play.
Everyone knows that this is my day.

Running Barefoot Through My Mind

My toes are squeezed in shoes that bind,
So I'll run barefoot through my mind;
And think of all mem'ries I dare
To gather thoughts from here and there.

I've watched you, Mom, with expert care,
And find your talents "Oh, so rare."
Now years have gone; the time has flown.
Into womanhood I have grown.

Seems yesterday . . . you combed my hair,
And buttoned up my dress with care.
You laced my shoes
And kissed each bruise.

You blend the gifts I scarcely know.
You helped me understand and grow.
Baking, sewing, ironing, and such,
Mom, you do have that special touch

There is no music or fine art,
To equal talents in your heart.
Because of all your special ways,
My time glides by in gold-filled days.

You wooed me with your tender art;
Now, Mom, you're the pride of my heart.
My toes are squeezed in shoes that bind,
So I'll run barefoot through my mind.

Serenity in Silhouettes

Autumn is coming to the shore,
But summer will return once more.
Soon you will hear the flapping wings;
Listen as a chirping bird sings.

They are the sounds of sad good-byes,
As great flocks in formation rise.
In perfect vees, they'll fly so high
Wings flap to echo their good-bye.

Autumn is coming to the shore,
But summer will return once more

Slipping Away

Believing is gone, compassion no more.
Creature of earth, that is all that she's for.
"Experiencing Mankind" is her gist.
Does human kindness really exist?

No hopes and dreams to brighten the way.
A fragile heart breaking every day.
Put forth with mellow accents in the sky,
And cutting expressions peaking so high.

Is it possible her hope is finished?
Could it be that her dreams are diminished?
Is it possible the limits have passed?
With the hurts being so deep and so vast.

Acceptance refused, her fighting no more.
Where can one go when the future is poor?
Where can one go when yesterday is lost?
Alone in her silence - - - Is this her cost?

As the surging of a billowing form
Of wind that's sinking from a rising storm,
Going down . . . all the way.
Guess there is nothing left for me to say!

Smit' the Glitter

Capture the magic of the simple life.
A cheerful embrace; away from the strife.
Harmony brings you a personal touch.
Sharing vitality, doesn't take much.

Smit' the glitter and the phony decor!
Really and truly - simple, bestows more.

Freshly cut grass, and white picket fences.
It's such a pleasure to use all five senses.
Persuading a frown, into a smile,
Making 'thingumajigs', all worthwhile.

Smit' the glitter and the phony decor!
Really and truly - simple, bestows more.

That Old Streetlight

Come! I'll share a childhood I once knew.
I'll bring old memories to share with you.
It's always such a refreshing pleasure
To turn simple things into a treasure.

Tonight in front of my house I did see
A streetlight that brought an old memory.
As if someone sharpened a camera lens
I recalled the days with childhood friends.

This treasure in front of my house so bright
Reminded me of a long ago light.
A single dim, bug-covered bulb embraced
Under a dark green covered shaded case.

The streetlight which lured me into the night,
Brings cherished memories of such delight.
The glare that enticed the fireflies glow.
I would catch them briefly, then let them go.

Here under the streetlight dreams are most clear.
With precious images arising near.
A sidewalk reflects little jagged cracks
With chalk markings that line the hopscotch tracks.

You came and shared a childhood I knew.
The streetlight that brought me to de ja vu.
Yet still somehow these images must end
This imagination shared with a friend.

The Dawn of Day

I arise in the morning to steal the dawn
Where all the heavy dew lay,
And savor it to last as long as I can.
With the breath of morning's glow
I can see the splendor of achievement.
Like the calm of a storm
And the bearer of cheer,
The breezes come rippling by,
Weaving a soft song to open my day.
Of all the wonder in the morning's magic
With all the blessings of nature's glory,
I rise with this daybreak to steal the dawn
Where the heavy dew lay across the quiet country morn.
A breeze from dawns sweetness blows
And knows a thousand ways to please.
So I pack up my treasures
To store them inside.
I welcome the dawn unveiling daybreak.

"The Tease of Blues and Greens"

Like the deep blue skies in heaven above,
The distant echoing sounds from afar
Brought back the pain and passion of my love.

So I asked within my heart where you are,
And felt the warmth like the suns golden light
So haunting, so wanting, and so bizarre.

The green of the tall trees came within sight.
As I felt a whiff of the warm sky breeze
Painting a masterpiece in early night.

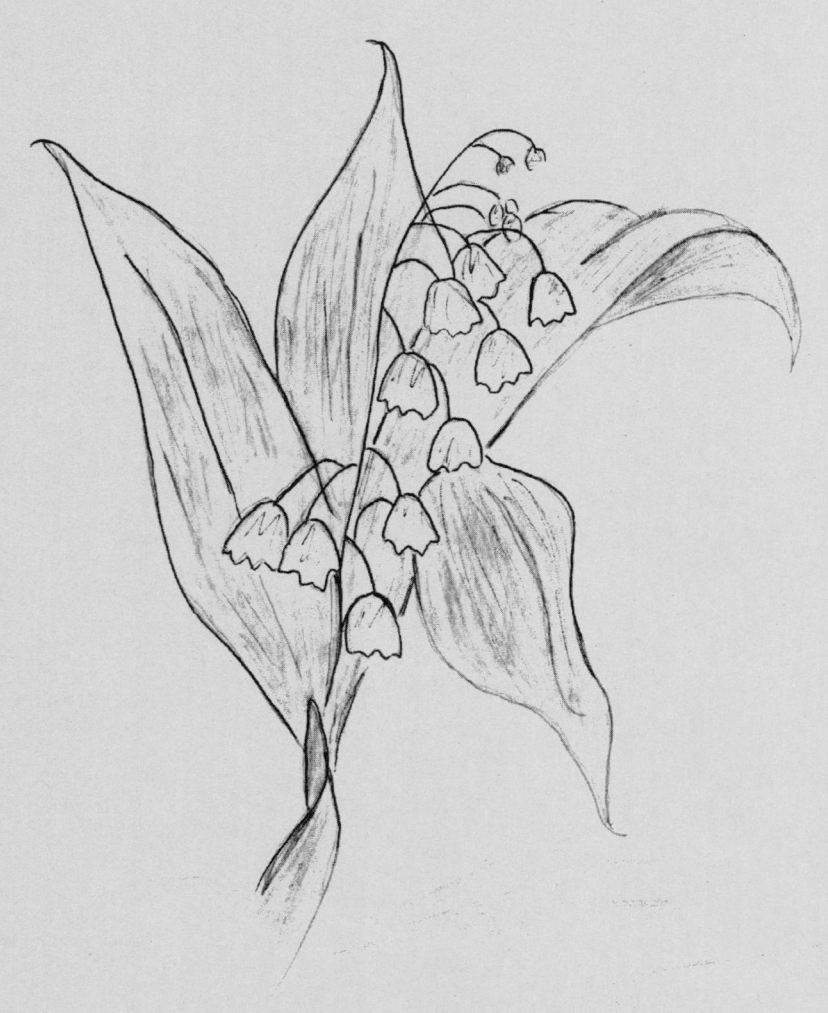

Thoughts

Thoughts dance in my head,
like drops of water
in a hot fry pan.

Time-Machine

A call to enter a "time-machine" seemed
Unmistaken a wish - a dream I knew.
To lend a sweeping view of what I dreamed,
As hinged doors opened time reversed on cue.

I walked a mile far down a path of wood.
My heart recalled a sentimental time,
And heard the chatter in the neighborhood.
My field of vision was of brief sublime.

I heard and savored sounds of life's echo,
And silently slipped through the wood screen door.
I paused under a canopy shadow
And being careful of things I adore.

Afar I can see just where I began.
I'm glad I lived when days were a pleasure.
With long anxious steps I joyfully ran
To capture my dream of life's past treasure.

Tomorrow, Let's Do It Again?

Stock market up,
Stock market down.
One day a smile,
Next day a frown.

Invest, Invest
The broker says.
Buy and Buy!
No! . . Sell and Sell!

Money gained,
Money lost
Money won!
Is this fun?

Gainers, losers!
Insiders, outsiders!
Nasdaq and Dow.
Holy Cow!

You laugh! You cry!
Kiss your money good-bye.
Then ask in pain
Tomorrow, let's do it over again?

Walking on the Beach

As the tide breaks on the shore,
I watch it ebb and flow;
As memories held dear
So fondly come and go!

Watching the Sea

Did you ever sit on the beach watching the sea?
Capturing it's moods and the smell of it.
The feel of it in the air.
The softness of it on a quiet morning,
And it's fury during a storm.
Did you ever listen to the sound of it?
Like a heart beating.
Did you ever see a wave climbing and whipping high and free?
Or the beauty of a small wave rippling like a simple, delicate flower
Unfurling petal by petal - then gently washing to shore.
Did you ever see the surfers threading their way between the waves?
Did you ever watch the horizon - shimmering against a fragile blue canvas sky?
What a beautiful gift God has given us!
Did you ever sit on the beach watching the sea?

Words

My words tumbling over each other
Like tumbleweeds breaking from it's roots
Rolling aimlessly into the wind,
Unable to verbalize my thoughts.

Then your words pierce me like an arrow.
Transferring a jolt of energy.
And I rejoice with a confidence.
Magically words become lyrics.

Like the escape of a bird in flight,
With the impact of a sudden wind
Rising against a blazing sunset,
I fly to the top. To the summit.

Youth Was Once So Sure

It's cold. She hears the faucet-tap dripping.
The room is bare. Her youth was once so sure.
The tap drips like a metronome's time-piece
Causing her to dream of the days gone by.
Like a delayed embryo awakened
She too feels the warmth of a vibrant life.
She recaptures a young vitality.
Coldness turns to warmth; time is in prelude.
Still drifting, she sighs and opens her eyes.
Her heart stutters a painful sensation.
The coldness returns. She feels her breath catch.
The dream is over. Youth was once so sure

Sunbeams

Written for my 11 yr old grand-daughter Casey

As morning slowly wakens me,
And shadows touch my windowpane,
I see a glowing light come through.

A sunbeam dances in the air.
She dashes high. She peeps through rays.
She taps my face to my amaze!

She sits upon my pillowcase.
Bright spears of arrows fill my room
As radiant beams lift my heart.

They greet me on this early morn,
Adorning such magnificence.
As morning slowly wakens me.